WATER

Written by Alex Hall

I0805961

ELEMENTS

Gareth Stevens PUBLISHING

Please visit our website, www.garethstevens.com. For a free color catalog of all our high-quality books, call toll free 1-800-542-2595 or fax 1-877-542-2596.

Published in 2025 by
Gareth Stevens Publishing
2544 Clinton St.
Buffalo, NY 14224

Written by:
Alex Hall

Edited by:
Rebecca Phillips-Bartlett

Designed by:
Ker Ker Lee

Cataloging-in-Publication Data

Names: Hall, Alex.
Title: Water / Alex Hall.
Description: Buffalo, NY : Gareth Stevens Publishing, 2025. | Series: Elements | Includes glossary and index.
Identifiers: ISBN 9781482468601 (pbk.) | ISBN 9781482468618 (library bound) | ISBN 9781482468625 (ebook)
Subjects: LCSH: Water--Juvenile literature. | Four elements (Philosophy)--Juvenile literature.
Classification: LCC GB662.3 H355 2025 | DDC 553.7--dc23

Printed in the United States of America

CPSIA compliance information: Batch #CW25GS: For further information contact Gareth Stevens at 1-800-542-2595.

Find us on

Photo Credits – Images are courtesy of Shutterstock.com, with thanks to Getty Images, Thinkstock Photo, and iStockphoto.

Recurring images – gravity_point.
Cover – CK Foto, Valentina Shilkina, MD_style.
2–3 – Stanislavskyi. 4–5 – Mayabuns, SP shutter.
6–7 – Maximillian cabinet, Gorloff-KV, Mike Pellinni, Valerii_M, George Trumpeter. 8–9 – StockBURIN. 10–11 – fizkes, Rozhnovskaya Tanya, JOKE_PHATRAPONG.
12–13 – Rich Carey, Lorna Roberts. 14–15 – Mimadeo, mTaira.
16–17 – Moshe EINHORN, Sergi Lopez Roig.
18–19 – KalininStudios, encierro. 20–21 – Evgeny Atamanenko, EpicStockMedia.
22–23 – Ikunl, zirconicusso.

CONTENTS

Words that look like <u>this</u> can be found in the glossary on page 24.

ESSENTIAL ELEMENTS

The four elements are water, earth, fire, and air. Each element has its own important job. Life on our planet would not be possible without them. Together, these elements keep the world in balance.

These elements are so important that they are known as the essential elements.

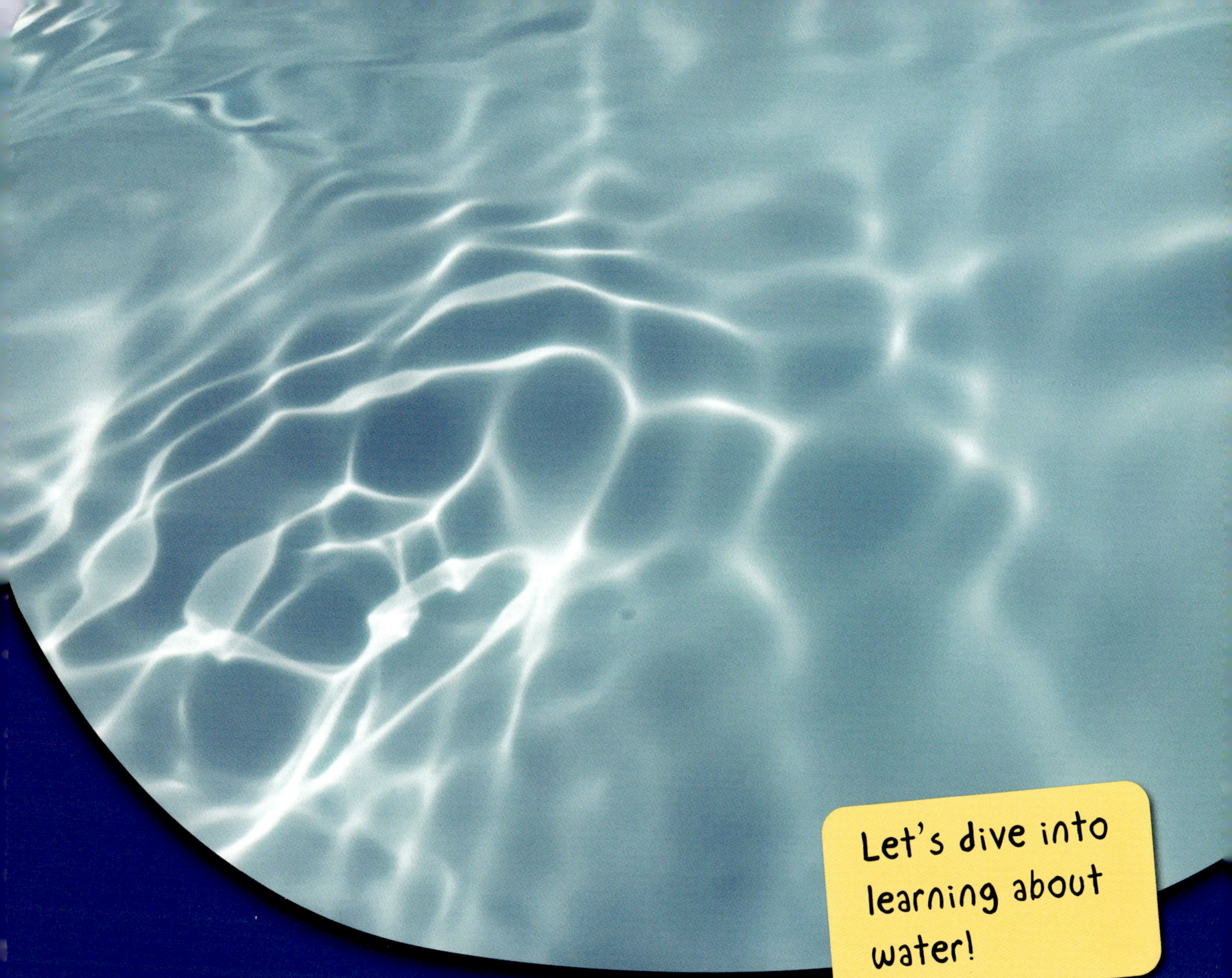

Let's dive into learning about water!

The stuff that fills up a bath is called water. People use it every day for many things. Even your body is mostly made up of water. There is so much to discover about water.

WHAT IS WATER?

ice

Water is a liquid. A liquid is a kind of matter that flows. When water freezes, it becomes ice. Ice is a solid. Water can also become a gas called water vapor when it gets hot.

vapor

Water is the only element that can be a solid, liquid, or gas.

Water is in every river, lake, and ocean around the world. Water covers almost three-quarters of the planet. This means there is more water on Earth than there is land.

THE WATER CYCLE

The water cycle is the journey that water takes on Earth.

A lot of water is found in rivers and oceans. The sun's heat turns this water into vapor. The vapor moves upward and makes clouds.

If the water freezes, it becomes snow.

Inside clouds, the vapor turns into water droplets.

After a while, the droplets get too heavy to stay in the cloud. They fall to the ground as rain or snow.

WATERS OF LIFE

Humans, plants, and animals use water to stay alive. All living things need water. Drinking water helps our bodies break down food. It also helps oxygen flow in our bodies.

We use water to clean our clothes and wash our bodies. Soap mixes with water to help clean things. Washing with water and soap keeps us healthy. Without it, we would also be very smelly!

washing clothes

Can you think of something else you wash with water?

washing hands

WILD WATER

Water is home to many animals, such as fish. Millions of fish live in the lakes, rivers, and oceans around the world. Fish breathe underwater using body parts called gills.

Fish use their gills to get oxygen from water.

A habitat is the place an animal or plant lives.

There are many different underwater habitats. Some fish live in saltwater habitats such as the ocean. Other fish can only live in fresh water found in rivers and lakes.

TSUNAMIS

Tsunamis are natural disasters. Natural disasters are events caused by nature, not by humans. Sometimes, movement under the ocean causes a lot of water to move in large waves. This is called a tsunami.

Tsunamis can travel long distances. If tsunamis reach land, they can be very dangerous. Tsunamis can be powerful enough to destroy buildings and cause people to lose their homes.

TSUNAMI SAFETY

HOW TO STAY SAFE IN A TSUNAMI ALERT

- Look out for signs of a tsunami, such as the water pulling back, and warnings on the radio and TV, or warning sirens.
- Go to higher ground so tsunami waves cannot reach you.

SAFE SWIMMING

HOW TO STAY SAFE IN THE WATER:

- Take swimming lessons so you can move well in the water.
- Only swim in places that are meant for swimming and have a lifeguard.

A lifeguard looks after people who are swimming to keep them safe.

WATER POLLUTION

Water pollution is when a lot of garbage and harmful chemicals are in the water. Polluted water is bad for all living things.

Some people litter. Littering means dropping garbage on the ground and leaving it there. This garbage often ends up in rivers and oceans. Always throw out your garbage in the right cans or bins to help stop water pollution.

Recycling can help reduce, or lower, pollution.

SPLASH AND SURF

There are many fun activities that can be done in the water. Splashing in puddles is one way to enjoy water. It can make you wet or dirty, so wash your clothes afterwards.

Do you ever splash in puddles?

There are many sports that take place in the water. Surfing is a water sport. Surfing is when someone uses a board to ride waves in the ocean. It takes a lot of practice.

WONDERFUL WATER

Water covers most of Earth. It keeps all living things alive. We drink and wash with it every day. It is also home to all sorts of animals all over the world.

Water is a wonderful element for so many amazing reasons. It gives life to many things, but it can also be dangerous in some situations. Can you think of any other uses of water?

GLOSSARY

balance the state in which things exist in the correct amounts to keep things stable

balance matter that can be mixed with other matter to cause changes

gas matter that spreads out to fill any space available

oxygen a gas that living things need in order to live

recycling using something again to make something else

solid matter that is firm and does not change shape easily

INDEX